ST GABRIEL

OF OUR LADY OF SORROWS

PASSIONIST
A YOUTHFUL HERO OF SANCTITY

NOVENA

BY
JOANNAH LIGHT

TABLE OF CONTENT
INTRODUCTION

BACKGROUND ON ST. GABRIEL
OF OUR LADY OF SORROWS

Saint Gabriel hailed from a family of thirteen siblings. During his childhood, he engaged in typical activities such as having fun, attending school, playing, hunting, and acting, just like any ordinary boy. However, as he matured, a sense of incompleteness crept into his life. He sensed a divine calling, a beckoning from God to seek something more meaningful.

Soon, after a vision of Our Lady told him that what he was suspecting was true, that the interests of the world were not for him, he joined the Passionist Order. He became a priest and looked forward to a full life of service to Our Lord and Our Blessed Mother. His life was uneventful, devoted to prayer, sacrifice, and a devotion to Our Lady and the contemplation of her sorrows over the suffering of Jesus. He was still fun-loving and generous, and enjoyed helping others.

Following his ordination, Saint Gabriel of the Sorrowful Mother faced a challenging turn of events as he fell seriously ill with tuberculosis, ultimately leading to his untimely death. However, posthumously, numerous miracles were attributed to him, serving as a testament to his heavenly journey and his intercessory role for those seeking his aid. Notably, Saint Gemma Galgani experienced a miraculous cure after praying to him.

When Saint Gabriel was canonised, Pope Benedict XV highlighted him as an exemplary model for young people. Born in Assisi, Italy, in 1838 and baptised as Francis in honor of the revered St. Francis of Assisi, Saint Gabriel faced early adversity with the death of his mother when he was only four years old.

Despite his striking handsomeness and friendly demeanor , Francis harbored a deeper longing for God and the profound aspects of life. Even amidst a social and active life, he occasionally felt a sense of boredom that he couldn't articulate, driven by a strong desire for spiritual fulfilment.

Twice faced with near-death experiences due to illness, Francis promised Our Lady that he would enter religious life if she secured his recovery. Regrettably, he failed to uphold this promise on both occasions. However, a pivotal moment occurred when he encountered an image of the Sorrowful Mother during a procession. To Francis, it felt as if the Blessed Mother was directly addressing him, accompanied by a voice in his heart proclaiming, "Francis, the world is not for you anymore."

Unable to evade his calling any longer, Francis entered the Passionist monastery at the age of eighteen, adopting the name Gabriel of the Sorrowful Mother. His profound love for the Holy Eucharist and devotion to Mary, the Sorrowful Mother, became the cornerstones of his spiritual life. He immersed himself in contemplation of Jesus's passion, reflecting on the immense suffering the Lord endured for his sake.

As a member of the Passionist order, Gabriel immersed himself in the practice of two virtues, humility and obedience. Yet, it was his most dominant and strongest characteristic—joy—that set him apart. His infectious happiness radiated to those around him. Despite only spending four years in the Passionist order, Gabriel succumbed to tuberculosis on February 27, 1862, and was later canonised as a saint by Pope Benedict XV in 1920.

Gabriel's life serves as a lesson, emphasising the importance of not merely seeking good times but finding genuine joy and meaning. Families seeking guidance can turn to St. Gabriel for help in discovering authentic joy in their lives.

Born as Francis Possenti in the renowned town of Assisi, Italy, on March 1, 1838, he was the eleventh child in a family of thirteen. His father, holding roles as a civil and Church lawyer, served as a public official in the Papal states, which eventually became part of a unified Italy in 1859.

Despite enjoying the typical interests of boys his age, such as hunting, dancing, and theatre, Francis experienced a peculiar dissatisfaction with his otherwise happy and prosperous life. This discontentment found resolution when he felt a calling to the religious and priestly life. Joining the Congregation of the Passionists, a community dedicated to living and preaching the saving merits of Our Lord's passion and death, Francis took vows and adopted the religious name Gabriel of the Sorrowful One (or Sorrowful Mother).

A year before his anticipated ordination as a priest, Francis was stricken with tuberculosis and passed away on February 27, 1862, in the Passionist monastery at Gran Sasso in the Abruzzi region of Italy. Throughout his religious life, Gabriel exhibited faithfulness to prayer, love of sacrifice, heroic virtue, and an unwavering cheerful disposition despite his illness. Following his death, miraculous cures were attributed to his intercession.

Pope Benedict XV canonized Gabriel in 1920 and declared him the patron of Catholic youth. In 1959, Pope John XXIII designated him as the patron of the Abruzzi region, where e spent his final two years. The shrine at Gran Sasso remains one of Europe's more popular destinations for those seeking inspiration from St. Gabriel's life.

PURPOSE OF THE NOVENA OF

ST. GABRIEL OF OUR LADY OF

SORROWS

The purpose of the novena dedicated to St. Gabriel of the Sorrowful Mother is to engage in a nine-day period of prayer and reflection, seeking the intercession and inspiration of this saint.

Participants undertake this spiritual journey to draw closer to God, deepen their faith, and receive guidance in their lives .

The key objectives of the novena are:

1. Spiritual Growth: The novena offers an opportunity for individuals to grow spiritually by focusing on St. Gabriel's virtues, such as humility, obedience, and joy. Participants strive to emulate these qualities in their own lives.

2. Intercession: Participants seek St. Gabriel's intercession in their prayers, asking for his help in specific intentions, needs, or challenges they may be facing. Believers trust in the saint's connection with heaven and his willingness to intercede on their behalf.

3. Devotion to Our Lady: St. Gabriel had a deep devotion to the Sorrowful Mother, and the novena may also serve to strengthen participants' connections with Mary. The faithful may seek Mary's guidance and comfort, following St. Gabriel's example.

4. Reflection on Suffering and Sacrifice:St. Gabriel's contemplation of the passion of Jesus encourages participants to reflect on the meaning of suffering and sacrifice in their own lives. The novena may provide a space for believers to offer their challenges and sacrifices in union with Christ's suffering.

5. Joyful Christian Living: St. Gabriel's joyful disposition despite his trials serves as an inspiration for a joyful Christian life. The novena may aim to help individuals cultivate a sense of

joy rooted in faith, regardless of life's circumstances.

6. Model for Young People:As recommended by Pope Benedict XV, the novena may also emphasise St. Gabriel as a model for young people, encouraging them to navigate the challenges of life with faith, joy, and a commitment to serving God.

Ultimately, the novena is a dedicated period of prayer and reflection, fostering a deeper connection with God, St. Gabriel, and the broader Catholic faith community. Participants may use this time to seek spiritual guidance, express gratitude, and strengthen their commitment to living a life in accordance with Christian values.

Prayer to St. Gabriel of Our Lady of Sorrows

Opening Prayer:

Dear St. Gabriel of Our Lady of Sorrows,

As we embark on this sacred novena in your honor, we gather with hearts open to the grace and intercession you offer. You, who found solace in the Sorrowful Mother and embraced a life of humility, obedience, and joy, inspire us on our spiritual journey.

St. Gabriel, we seek your presence and guidance during these nine days of prayer. Help us to reflect on the virtues that marked your earthly journey and to draw closer to the divine purpose God has set for each of us.

In the midst of our joys and sorrows, may your example teach us to trust in the Lord's plan, finding meaning in every moment. May our hearts be open to the whispers of the Holy Spirit, guiding us towards a deeper relationship with God and a greater understanding of His will for our lives.

St. Gabriel, through your intercession, we lift up our intentions and needs [mention specific intentions]. Obtain for us the grace to persevere in faith, to find joy in sacrifice, and to grow in love for our Blessed Mother and our Lord Jesus Christ.

May this novena be a time of spiritual renewal, drawing us closer to the heart of God. We entrust our prayers to you, confident that you, dear saint, are a powerful advocate before the throne of grace.

St. Gabriel of Our Lady of Sorrows, pray for us. Amen.

DAY 1: VIRTUE OF HOPE

Reflection:

Dear St. Gabriel of Our Lady of Sorrows, on this first day of our novena, we turn our hearts to the virtue of hope. Like you, who discerned a divine calling and embraced a life of meaning, we seek to cultivate a hopeful spirit in our journey of faith.

Reflecting on the virtue of hope, we recognize it as the anchor of our souls, a confident expectation in God's promises. In moments of doubt and uncertainty, may we find inspiration in your life, dear saint, and trust in the providence of our Heavenly Father.

Scripture Readings:
1. Jeremiah 29:11: "For I know the plans I have for you, declares the LORD, plans for welfare and not for evil, to give you a future and a hope."

2. Romans 15:13: "May the God of hope fill you with all joy and peace in believing, so that by the power of the Holy Spirit you may abound in hope."
3. Psalm 39:7: "And now, O Lord, for what do I wait? My hope is in you."

Prayer for Hope:

Heavenly Father, source of all hope, we lift our hearts to You on this day, seeking the virtue of hope that St. Gabriel exemplified. In times of uncertainty and challenge, help us to anchor our trust in Your divine plan, knowing that You hold our future in Your hands.

St. Gabriel, you who found hope in the midst of life's mysteries, intercede for us before the throne of grace. May the Holy Spirit infuse our hearts with a hopeful spirit, enabling us to face each day with confidence in Your unfailing love.

Grant us the grace to persevere in hope, even when circumstances seem bleak. May our lives

reflect the radiant hope that comes from our faith in You. We entrust our aspirations and concerns to your intercession, St. Gabriel, confident that you walk with us on this journey.
In the name of the Father, and of the Son, and of the Holy Spirit.
Amen.

DAY 2: THE ANNUNCIATION

Meditation:

On this second day of our novena, let us reflect upon the profound moment of the Annunciation. Picture the scene: the humble Virgin Mary, visited by the Angel Gabriel, who brought news of the Savior's impending arrival. As we meditate on this sacred event, let us contemplate the obedience, faith, and humility that Mary and the Angel Gabriel exemplified.

In the silence of our hearts, may we open ourselves to the messages God sends our way, just as Mary did with grace and trust. May we, like St. Gabriel, be messengers of God's love and bearers of His good news in our own lives.

Scriptural Reflections:

1. Luke 1:26-38: The account of the Annunciation, where the Angel Gabriel announces to Mary that she will conceive and bear the Son of God.

2. Daniel 9:21-23: Reflecting on the role of the Angel Gabriel in delivering messages of great importance in the plan of salvation.
3. Luke 1:46-55: Mary's Magnificat, a hymn of praise and humility in response to the Annunciation.

Novena Prayer for the Intercession of St. Gabriel:

Dear St. Gabriel, Angel of the Annunciation and messenger of God's love, on this day dedicated to the momentous event of the Annunciation, we seek your intercession.

As you delivered the message of salvation to Mary, we ask you to intercede for us in our moments of need. Like Mary, help us to respond to God's call with obedience and faith. May we be open to the messages He sends into our lives, trusting in His divine plan.

St. Gabriel, messenger of joy, bring our intentions before the throne of God. Through your intercession, may we experience the grace of God's guidance and feel the presence of the Holy Spirit in our hearts.

Pray for us, St. Gabriel, that we may be open to God's will in our lives and bear witness to the good news of salvation. In your name, we seek this intercession.

In the name of the Father, and of the Son, and of the Holy Spirit.
Amen.

DAY 3: THE SORROWS OF MARY

Contemplation on the Seven Sorrows of

Mary:

As we enter the third day of our novena, let us turn our hearts to the deep sorrows that Mary, our Sorrowful Mother, experienced throughout her life. Contemplate the Seven Sorrows: **the prophecy of Simeon, the flight into Egypt, the loss of the Child Jesus in the Temple, the meeting of Jesus and Mary on the Way of the Cross, the Crucifixion, the taking down of Jesus' body from the Cross, and His burial.**
Take a moment to reflect on the profound sorrow Mary endured, and how she bore her pain with unwavering faith and love. Allow her example to inspire us in facing our own sorrows and challenges with grace and trust in God.

DEVOTIONAL PRAYERS FOR THOSE EXPERIENCING SORROW:

Prayer of Consolation:

Heavenly Father, in times of sorrow and distress, be our comfort and solace. We turn to You with open hearts, seeking the consoling embrace of Your love. Wrap us in Your tender mercy and grant us the strength to endure our trials, knowing that You are with us, even in our darkest moments.

Novena Prayer for Comfort and Solace :

Dear St. Gabriel, compassionate messenger of God, on this day dedicated to contemplating the sorrows of our Blessed Mother, we come to you seeking comfort and solace.

In moments of sorrow, be our guide and intercessor. Just as you found solace in the arms of the Sorrowful Mother, help us navigate the challenges and pains of life with grace and trust in God's providence.

St. Gabriel, advocate for those experiencing sorrow, we bring our burdens before you [mention specific intentions]. Through your intercession, may we find comfort, strength, and the peace that comes from placing our trust in the Divine.

Pray for us, St. Gabriel, that we may emerge from our sorrows with hearts uplifted and strengthened by the grace of God. In your name, we seek this intercession.

In the name of the Father, and of the Son, and of the Holy Spirit.

Amen.

DAY 4: THE PASSION OF CHRIST

Reflection on St. Gabriel's Devotion to the Passion :

On this fourth day of our novena, let us reflect on St. Gabriel's profound devotion to the Passion of Christ. St. Gabriel embraced the mystery of Christ's suffering, finding inspiration and purpose in meditating on the immense love and sacrifice embodied in the Passion.

Consider how St. Gabriel's contemplation of the Passion influenced his own life and choices. May his example inspire us to approach the challenges in our lives with a spirit of self-sacrifice, recognizing the redemptive power of Christ's suffering.

Scripture Passages on Christ's Suffering:

1. Isaiah 53:3-5: "He was despised and rejected by men, a man of sorrows and acquainted with grief... But he was pierced

for our transgressions; he was crushed for our iniquities."

2. Matthew 26:38-39: "Then he said to them, 'My soul is very sorrowful, even to death; remain here, and watch with me.' And going a little farther he fell on his face and prayed, saying, 'My Father, if it be possible, let this cup pass from me; nevertheless, not as I will, but as you will.'"

3. Philippians 2:8: "And being found in human form, he humbled himself by becoming obedient to the point of death, even death on a cross."

Novena Prayer for Strength in Times of Suffering:

Heavenly Father, as we delve into the mystery of Christ's Passion on this day of our novena, we recognize the depth of His love and sacrifice for us. Grant us the grace to draw strength from His suffering in times of our own trials and challenges.

St. Gabriel, who found inspiration in the Passion of Christ, we seek your intercession for strength in our moments of suffering. Help us to unite our hardships with the redemptive suffering of our Lord, knowing that through our trials, we may share in His resurrection.

In times of sorrow and pain, may we find comfort in the knowledge that Christ walks with us. St. Gabriel, advocate for those facing the cross, pray for us [mention specific intentions] and grant us the courage to persevere with unwavering faith.

Pray for us, St. Gabriel, that we may face our crosses with the same spirit of sacrifice and love that you and our Lord demonstrated. In your name, we seek this intercession.

In the name of the Father, and of the Son, and of the Holy Spirit.

Amen.

DAY 5: THE EUCHARIST

Consideration of St. Gabriel's Love for the Eucharist:

As we embark on the fifth day of our novena, let us reflect on St. Gabriel's profound love for the Eucharist. St. Gabriel found solace, inspiration, and deep communion with God through the Holy Eucharist. Consider how his devotion to the Blessed Sacrament enriched his spiritual life and fostered a profound sense of intimacy with Christ.

Contemplate how St. Gabriel's love for the Eucharist influenced his daily life and actions. May his example encourage us to approach the Eucharist with reverence, gratitude, and a longing for a deeper union with our Lord.

Eucharistic Prayers and Reflections:

1. John 6:35: "Jesus said to them, 'I am the bread of life; whoever comes to me shall not hunger, and whoever believes in me shall never thirst.'"
2. 1 Corinthians 11:23-26: St. Paul's account of the institution of the Eucharist, emphasising its significance in remembering and proclaiming the Lord's death.
3. St. Gabriel's Reflections on the Eucharist: Consider any writings or quotes from St. Gabriel that express his sentiments and reflections on the Holy Eucharist.

Novena Prayer for a Deeper Appreciation of the Eucharist:

Heavenly Father, as we meditate on St. Gabriel's love for the Eucharist, we stand before the mystery of Your presence in the Blessed Sacrament. Open our hearts to receive the grace of a deeper appreciation for this sacred gift.

St. Gabriel, who found nourishment for his soul in the Eucharist, intercede for us. Help us to approach the altar with the same reverence and love that you did. May our participation in the Eucharist strengthen our faith, deepen our love for Christ, and foster unity with our brothers and sisters in the Body of Christ.

Grant us the grace to recognize the real presence of Jesus in the Eucharist and to approach this sacred banquet with humility and awe. St. Gabriel, advocate for a profound Eucharistic devotion, pray for us [mention specific intentions] and lead us closer to the heart of our Lord.

Pray for us, St. Gabriel, that we may experience the transformative power of the Eucharist in our lives. In your name, we seek this intercession.

In the name of the Father, and of the Son, and of the Holy Spirit.

Amen.

DAY 6: ZEAL FOR THE SALVATION OF SOULS

Exploration of St. Gabriel's Zeal for Souls:

As we enter the sixth day of our novena, let us delve into St. Gabriel's fervent zeal for the salvation of souls. St. Gabriel, inspired by his love for God and humanity, dedicated himself to the mission of spreading the Gospel and leading souls to Christ. Reflect on how his passion for evangelization influenced his actions and interactions.

Consider the ways in which St. Gabriel's zeal for souls can serve as a model for our own lives. May his example inspire us to actively engage in the work of bringing others closer to the love and mercy of our Savior.

Scriptural Passages on Evangelization:

1. Matthew 28:19-20: "The Great Commission, where Jesus instructs His disciples to go and make disciples of all nations.

2. Mark 16:15: "And he said to them, 'Go into all the world and proclaim the gospel to the whole creation.'"

3. 2 Timothy 4:2: "Preach the word; be ready in season and out of season; reprove, rebuke, and exhort, with complete patience and teaching."

Novena Prayer for Missionary Zeal:

Heavenly Father, on this day of our novena dedicated to exploring St. Gabriel's zeal for the salvation of souls, we humbly seek Your guidance and grace. Grant us the same fervor that burned in the heart of St. Gabriel, inspiring him to work tirelessly for the Kingdom.

St. Gabriel, zealous herald of the Gospel, intercede for us. Help us to embrace a missionary spirit, sharing the Good News of Jesus Christ with those around us. May our words and actions reflect the love and mercy of our Savior, drawing souls closer to the embrace of Your grace.

Grant us the courage to be bold witnesses for Christ, following in the footsteps of St. Gabriel. Pray for us [mention specific intentions], that our

efforts in evangelization may bear fruit for the glory of Your name.
St. Gabriel, advocate for the salvation of souls, inspire us to be instruments of Your divine love.
In your name, we seek this intercession.
In the name of the Father, and of the Son, and of the Holy Spirit.
Amen.

DAY 7: HUMILITY AND OBEDIENCE

Reflection on St. Gabriel's Virtues of Humility and Obedience:

On this seventh day of our novena, let us reflect on the virtues of humility and obedience exemplified by St. Gabriel. Despite his popularity and charm, St. Gabriel embraced a humble and obedient spirit, acknowledging his dependence on God's will.

Consider how St. Gabriel's life reflects these virtues and how they allowed him to align himself with the divine plan. Reflect on moments in your own life where humility and obedience can deepen your connection with God.

PRAYERS FOR HUMILITY AND OBEDIENCE :

Prayer for Humility :

Heavenly Father, grant us the grace of true humility. May we recognize our dependence on You and acknowledge Your sovereignty in our lives. Help us to see ourselves through Your eyes and to embrace a humble spirit that mirrors the example of St. Gabriel.

Prayer for Obedience:

Lord Jesus, teach us the beauty of obedience to Your will. May we listen attentively to Your voice and follow Your commands with a heart open to Your guidance. St. Gabriel's obedience inspires us; may we, too, submit ourselves to Your divine plan with joy and trust.

NOVENA PRAYER FOR THE GRACE TO FOLLOW GOD'S WILL:

Dear Heavenly Father, on this day of our novena dedicated to the virtues of humility and obedience, we implore Your guidance and grace. Through the example of St. Gabriel, we aspire to cultivate humble hearts and obedient spirits.

St. Gabriel, model of humility and obedience, intercede for us. Pray that we may embrace a posture of humility, acknowledging our weaknesses and surrendering our will to Yours. Grant us the grace to obey Your commands with joy, trusting in the wisdom of Your divine plan.

As we navigate the path of life, may we find solace in Your will and experience the freedom that comes from humble submission. We entrust our desires and intentions to Your loving care, seeking Your will above all else.

St. Gabriel, advocate for humble and obedient hearts, inspire us to follow God's will with unwavering trust. In your name, we seek this intercession.

In the name of the Father, and of the Son, and of the Holy Spirit.

Amen.

DAY 8: DEVOTION TO OUR LADY OF SORROWS

Overview of St. Gabriel's Devotion to the Sorrowful Mother:

As we enter the eighth day of our novena, let us delve into St. Gabriel's deep devotion to Our Lady of Sorrows. St. Gabriel found solace and inspiration in contemplating the sorrows of the Blessed Virgin Mary, seeking a profound connection with the Sorrowful Mother.

Reflect on how St. Gabriel's devotion to Our Lady of Sorrows influenced his spiritual life and actions. Consider the ways in which this devotion can serve as a source of strength and comfort in our own lives.

Prayers to Our Lady of Sorrows:
-Hail Mary :

Hail Mary, full of grace, the Lord is with thee; blessed art thou among women, and blessed is the fruit of thy womb, Jesus. Holy Mary, Mother of God, pray for us sinners, now and at the hour of our death. Amen.
- Stabat Mater (Sequence in Honor of Our Lady of Sorrows):
Stabat Mater dolorosa iuxta Crucem lacrimosa, dum pendebat Filius . (At the cross, her station keeping, stood the mournful Mother weeping, close to Jesus to the last.)

Novena Prayer for Mary's Intercession:

Dear St. Gabriel, on this day focused on your devotion to Our Lady of Sorrows, we turn to the Sorrowful Mother with trust and hope. As you found strength and inspiration in contemplating Mary's sorrows, intercede for us before her maternal heart.
Our Lady of Sorrows, pray for us [mention specific intentions]. In moments of trial and sorrow, may we find solace in your compassionate gaze and draw strength from the example of St. Gabriel. Through your intercession, may we experience the loving presence of your Son, Jesus Christ.
St. Gabriel, who found a companion in Our Lady of Sorrows, guide us to deepen our relationship with the Sorrowful Mother. Pray that, like you, we may be drawn closer to Christ through her intercession.
In the name of the Father, and of the Son, and of the Holy Spirit.

Amen.

DAY 9: FINAL REFLECTION AND CLOSING PRAYER

SUMMATION OF THE NOVENA JOURNEY:

As we approach the final day of our novena, let us take a moment to reflect on the journey we have undertaken in the footsteps of St. Gabriel of Our Lady of Sorrows. Over these nine days, we have explored the virtues, passions, and devotions that marked St. Gabriel's spiritual life. We have sought inspiration from his example, turning our hearts toward God in prayer, reflection, and gratitude.

Consider the insights gained from St. Gabriel's life, the virtues he embodied, and the lessons he teaches us. Reflect on the ways in which this novena has deepened your connection with God and how you can carry the spirit of St. Gabriel into your daily life.

Final Prayer and Thanksgiving to St. Gabriel:

Dear St. Gabriel of Our Lady of Sorrows, as we conclude this novena dedicated to your life and legacy, we come before you with hearts filled with gratitude. Thank you for being our guide, intercessor, and companion on this spiritual journey.

In these nine days, we have reflected on your virtues, contemplated the mysteries of faith, and sought your intercession in moments of need. As we close this novena, we entrust our intentions to your care, confident that you, dear saint, walk with us on our journey of faith.

St. Gabriel, messenger of joy, intercede for us and obtain for us the graces we seek [mention specific intentions]. May the lessons learned from your life continue to inspire us to live with humility, joy, and a deep devotion to God and His Mother.

As we bid farewell to this novena, we carry the lessons of your life in our hearts. Pray for us, St. Gabriel, that we may follow your example and live lives pleasing to God.

In the name of the Father, and of the Son, and of the Holy Spirit.

Amen.

Appendix

St. Gabriel of Our Lady of Sorrows, we turn to you, seeking guidance and companionship on our path of faith. Inspire us to embody the virtues of humility, joy, and devotion that defined your life. Through your intercession, draw us nearer to the heart of God and the compassionate gaze of our Sorrowful Mother. Pray for us, St. Gabriel, that we may emulate your example and discover solace in the sorrows of Mary. Amen.

Litany of Our Lady of Sorrows:

Lord, have mercy on us.

Christ, have mercy on us.
Lord, have mercy on us.
Christ, hear us.
Christ, graciously hear us.
God the Father of Heaven, have mercy on us.
God the Son, Redeemer of the world, have mercy on us.
God the Holy Spirit, have mercy on us.
Holy Trinity, one God, have mercy on us.
Holy Mary, pray for us.
Holy Mother of God, pray for us.
Holy Virgin of Virgins, pray for us.
Mother most sorrowful, pray for us.
Mother most merciful, pray for us.
Mother most loving, pray for us.
Mother of Christ, pray for us.
Mother of divine grace, pray for us.
Mother of our Savior, pray for us.
Virgin most prudent, pray for us.
Virgin most venerable, pray for us.
Virgin most renowned, pray for us.
Virgin most powerful, pray for us.
Virgin most merciful, pray for us.
Virgin most faithful, pray for us.

Concluding Prayer:

O God, in whose Passion, according to the prophecy of Simeon, a sword of sorrow pierced through the most sweet soul of the glorious Virgin and Mother Mary, grant that we, who commemorate and reverence her sorrows, may experience the blessed effect of Your Passion. Through Christ our Lord. Amen.